Audacious Prayers for World Changers

Live and Pray Out Loud

Jade Simmons

Cover Design by Stuart Cottrell

Photography by Lisa-Marie Mazzucco

Printed in the United States of America

First Printing, 2015

Jade Media Publishing
www.jademedia.org

ISBN-13: 978-1511598125

Dedication

To my fearless and peerless mother, Loretta Smalls, who taught me to believe big and pray hard. Every fruit I bring forth is because of the seeds you have planted.

Table of Contents

vi

Foreword

In my desire to better know and serve God, I have read many devotionals and daily prayer guides. Some are designed to help us "get through" a recently encountered challenge, while others help us steadily develop into mature believers.

All of them have been valuable in my personal journey. However, very few deliberately inspire you to meet life's greatest challenge—to dare become the unique world-changer God created you to be, or to make your life count, right now! Jade Simmons has done exactly that.

Prayer is the adventure of a lifetime! As someone has wisely suggested, it not only changes things, it also changes the 'pray-er,' or the one who does the praying. The right prayers have the power to enlist heaven's assistance to help us discover and then unlock the incredibly gifted individual hidden within us. That person, occasionally sensed but seldom seen, is the real you--the person you were actually meant to be.

God created you to be an accomplished champion and to perform unusual exploits. Quietly that person within you waits to be released into the extraordinary destiny He specifically intended you to experience. The greatest tragedy of all is to resign ourselves to a life of meaningless desperation or attempt to silence that daring voice that challenges us to rise higher. As believers, created in God's image and likeness, we were meant to do so much more. Prayer is designed to interact with Heaven and make things happen!

In *Audacious Prayers*, Jade has given us words to meditate and pray daily for the next thirty-one days. It's a way to forever change our lives by connecting the dreamer and visionary within us to the God who first gives, and then fulfills our dreams and visions.

Such prayers can supply a wealth of templates that teach us it's okay to ask and believe God for more than just barely surviving until we're rewarded at the end of life's journey. The petitions Jade talks about will leave such a mark on this world, our lives will truly make a difference in a time when it really matters. When linked with faith and boldness, prayer can open an entirely new dimension for those who will imitate Oliver Twist by lifting their bowls to God and pleading, "More, Sir!"

Jade is an accomplished, world class concert pianist, an inspiring transformational speaker, and life coach. She and her husband, Jahrell, are both highly motivated and successful achievers of dreams. Together, they have discovered the empowerment of a limitless God whom they faithfully serve with joy and gladness. With the Apostle Paul, this couple has discovered that they, too, can do all things! I am honored to have this family as part of our team.

Senior Pastor Dr. R. Heard
Christian Tabernacle
Houston, Texas

Acknowledgments

To my husband Jahrell, my number one partner in life, my tireless supporter: I could not have completed this or anything else I go after without you. In you lay my greatest blessings.

A special thank you to Dr. Fred Jones, attorney, author, speaker and Publishing Strategist who embraced Audacious Prayers so wholeheartedly and determined alongside me to get it out and into the world.

www.DrFredJones.com

Audacious

adjective au·da·cious \ȯ-ˈdā-shəs\

: very confident and daring : very bold and surprising or shocking

1a : intrepidly daring : adventurous b: recklessly bold : rash

2 contemptuous of law, religion, or decorum: insolent

3 marked by originality and verve

Why Pray Audaciously?

It is impossible to live powerfully on this earth without having faith that we're here for a reason, that there's more to life than stuff and things and status, that maybe just maybe we're created to be downright incredible. I'm a Christian, I pray to Jesus and believe Him to be the Son of God who died for our sins. The God I pray to is not only the One who made the heavens and the earth, but He also made me and my destiny. People who share that belief will love what comes next in these prayers; they'll recognize the biblical premises. But who else is this devotional for? Anyone who wants to believe bigger, who understands there must be something bigger than themselves at play, who know they were created to be bigger and work for a larger cause beyond themselves.

This book is for world changers in action and in the making. So why pray audaciously? We do so because God told us to. What is more audacious then Him telling us to command HIM?!

Isaiah 45:11 (KJV)

Thus saith the LORD, the Holy One of Israel, and his Maker, "Ask Me of things to come concerning My sons, and concerning the work of my hands command ye Me."

That doesn't make us the boss of God. We can't strong-arm Him. His ways are set. But what He's telling us here is to know His will and His word so we can partner with Him on earth to see it through. When we know His word, we can pray what He already said is on it's way. In our own lives, we must pray what He's shown us to be true and then we'll be privy to the manifestation of those things in our lives. How exciting is that!

Exodus 34:10 (NIV)

Then the LORD said: "I am making a covenant with you. Before all your people I will do wonders never before done in any nation in all the world. The people you live among will see how awesome is the work that I, the LORD, will do for you."

The connotation of requiring ourselves, both men and women, to be extraordinary in as many areas possible has gotten a lot of negative flack. It's often alluded to as a bad or unattainable thing, as too much pressure to be putting on ourselves. But the truth is that I believe God has called us to be more than mere mortals. Being super human shouldn't be draining, it should be empowering if pursued correctly. It doesn't have to be linked to arrogance, ego or hard-headedness, but there is a recklessly bold, willful nature required when it comes to meeting challenges head on. That's what intrepidly daring world changers do, they greet challenges on purpose and with gusto.

At the same time, much of being super human requires a type of surrender that is probably next to impossible for the average high-octane human to embrace. Being superhuman costs you. It costs you your doubt, your negativity and ultimately your life. By "your life" I mean that you have to give up the comfort of being ordinary and you'll need to become almost contemptuous towards status quo. You'll need to give up your childhood dreams in favor of God's fully formed dreams for you. You have to not only give into, but ultimately look forward to the momentum of change and transition. When you do this, failures will still hurt, but they'll start to feel more like priceless lessons instead of devastating dead ends. Coasting will begin to annoy you and you'll begin to greet turbulence with an all-knowing expectation that something great and powerful, known as Level Next, is on the horizon. People and circumstances will still throw darts at you, but now you're maneuvering around them like Neo in the Matrix (Google it, young'uns)!

A Super Human World Changer is an ordinary person with extraordinary vision, extraordinary dreams, extraordinary work ethic and an extraordinary belief that God will not leave them hanging.

To become Super Human, we must also pray in an extraordinary way...every day. Some people are going to think these prayers are audacious and possibly boastful. And they'll be right. You should have the audacity to believe you can achieve incredible things and you should be boastful that your God is able to equip you for the challenge. I dare you to pray this way everyday from here on out. I double dog dare you!

This devotional is designed with the extraordinary in mind, for those looking to learn how to live and pray out loud. It's for people ready to change their language in a bold way, to revolutionize their relationship with God. It's also for people who really do believe they can move mountains with God behind them and behind their words. **Read and focus on one prayer each day. I dare you to read it out loud so your ears and your mind and your heart can be bowled over by the audaciousness you're speaking. Fill in the accompanying lists. Go in order or in any order you want. Spend your day aware of the things you asked for and watch closely to see how God manifests them over time. Take note of those manifestations. When the month ends, start over!** Part of praying differently will involve seeing the world around you differently. You'll know your praying is effective because it will start to feel like you can literally scale buildings, see through walls and predict what's coming next. I call that "Zooming". Most comfortingly, you'll begin to feel less and less fear, anxiety will become rare. Instead, those negative emotions will be replaced with a steadfastness of faith in an unshakeable God that you'll know without a shadow of a doubt is in your corner. This is what is required of world changers. They have to be in it to win it for the long haul. If you want to change the world, you must first change your mode of operation.

Day 1: A Prayer for the Courage to Go After Extraordinary Exploits

Daniel 11:32 (KJV)

And such as do wickedly against the covenant shall he corrupt by flatteries: but the people that do know their God shall be strong, and carry out great exploits.

I have to be honest. Thanks to my parents and the way God made me, I never learned how to dream small. I've only always envisioned myself going after big things, never small potatoes. In the process of living audaciously, you'll meet people who tell you to start being "realistic". Often with good intentions, they'll beg you to make Plan B's, plead with you not to bite off more than you can chew, they'll ask you if you really think what you're going after is really possible. What I realized a while ago is that when they ask that last question it comes from their own place of unbelief. They don't believe *they* could ever do what you're going after, so out of their own fear they implore you. NEVER BE IMPLORED BY SOMEONE ELSE'S FEAR. NEVER. We're created not just to survive, not just to live, but to chase the extraordinary. I know this because our God is extraordinary and we're supposed to chase Him full out. Pray like this and you just might catch Him.

1

Father God, the King of Great Exploits, the Maker of Miracles, the One who calls things that be not as though they were, I receive my higher calling. I'm not called to be ordinary, or to stay at status quo, or to be easily satisfied. I'm not designed to think small, or take baby steps, or even be reasonable when it comes to my faith in You. What I know that I know that I know is that You made me this way. Others don't have to understand me, they just have to back out of my way and watch me work in Your name. This audacity, this boldness, this disbelief of limitations, this unquenchable quest to do extraordinary things in Your name is the "it" trait You've blessed me with and I ask You now to never let this flame die. Keep me hungry, thirsty and committed to literally changing the world starting with the corner I'm in today. Make me excited about rising to the challenge, keep me focused on the impossible and partner with me to make it so. The more exploits I complete, turn the spotlight brighter and brighter on You, Lord, my Holy Partner-in-Crime. I'm ready to move mountains with the sound of my voice, to heal sickness with the wave of a hand, to change the atmosphere of a room simply by walking into it. Keep me strong and capable of finishing what I start and make each task greater than the next so that the world will see You helped me rise to the challenge. I'm ready to walk on water hand-in-hand with You, I'm ready to calm raging seas, I'm ready to warm apathetic hearts, cleanse corrupted systems, topple evil deeds, change lives, open the door to destinies once thought lost. I'm ready to do greater works than You since You told me that was my inheritance. I understand what comes with being Your son or daughter, it means I'm grafted into a supernatural lineage. With that type of blood now flowing in my veins, I can't help but make great exploits my mode of operation.

Give me what You have for me today and I will not let You down. Jesus, I trust You to not leave me standing ashamed at Your absence. Ride with me Father God. In Your Holy Name, Amen.

Boldly list your most extraordinary dreams. Don't put anything small here, list only the exploits you could never accomplish on your own. The things you will achieve once you become completely and utterly God-powered are:

_____

_____

_____

_____

_____

_____

_____

_____

_____

_____

_____

_____

_____

_____

_____

_____

_____

_____

_____

Day 2: A Prayer for New Senses

Exodus 4:11 (NIV)

The LORD said to him, "Who gave human beings their mouths? Who makes them deaf or mute? Who gives them sight or makes them blind? Is it not I, the LORD?

You're pretty smart on your own, but often your own ambitions and the trials of life can mess with the effectiveness of your radar. You'll need to be sure you're seeing straight. God has an app for that.

Father, give me new eyes so that I might see as You do, new ears so I can hear as You hear. Give me a new mouth and tongue so that I can speak only as You would have me speak and more importantly, so that I'll know when to be quiet. Give me a new heart so that I can feel as deeply and compassionately as You do about people. Give me a nose that sniffs things out; help me quickly discern truth from falsehood so that I'll avoid bad relationships and messy business partnerships. If I'm already in one, give me the sense and the know-how to get out quickly and with the least damage done possible. And while You're giving things out, I'll take a new mind as well so that my thoughts can be Yours, which I know are far better than mine anyway. Give me new arms and hands so that everything I touch will turn to gold. Make me the new Midas, not just in the material sense (though there's nothing wrong with that, either), but when it comes to people and situations I'll have a special power to make things right and whole, and yes, profitable, too. Make it so my touch can be a blessing to others and please make my embrace a shelter for those that need it most. Give me new feet so I can walk only where You want me to go and won't get tripped up on a rocky path of my own making. Make me sick to my stomach when I unwittingly wind up in bad environments or dangerous situations. Give me the wits to get out smartly and quickly. With Godspeed, I ask for this in Your Holy Name, Amen.

Take note of your sharpest senses and make a point to rely on them often. But also take the time to find out where your senses have become or have always been dull. Do you find yourself in the same situations because you keep missing the same thing over and over? Ask God to repair that tool, to fix your compass in that area and watch it get sharpened as the days go by.

.

Day 3: A Prayer for Discernment

1 Kings 3:11-15 (NIV)

So God said to him, "Since you have asked for this and not for long life or wealth for yourself, nor have asked for the death of your enemies, but for discernment in administering justice, I will do what you have asked. I will give you a wise and discerning heart, so that there will never have been anyone like you, nor will there ever be. Moreover, I will give you what you have not asked for—both riches and honor—so that in your lifetime you will have no equal among kings. And if you walk in my ways and obey my statutes and commands as David your father did, I will give you a long life." Then Solomon awoke—and he realized it had been a dream.

Oh, but it was more than a dream and Solomon knew it because the next day he threw a celebration in honor of this promise which he expected to come to pass. Solomon knew firsthand that wisdom is not earned by just being on earth for a long time. True wisdom is granted. You have to want to be gifted with knowledge beyond what you can attain on your own. People who think they're the giver of their own wisdom by way of studying will always be one step behind. <u>Have the humility to ask for knowledge, wisdom and insight beyond what you can grant yourself.</u> Discernment is one grant you want to be sure to apply for.

Father God, I know that I will never ever need to consult a psychic or call up the dead because I know that what You have to show me is far more invaluable than the slivers of half truths any medium can offer. You are going to enable me to use that large portion of my brain that most humans never access. That, in combination with access to the gift of the Holy Spirit and a finely tuned soul, is going to make it look to some like I'm always 10 steps ahead. It will look like I know what's coming, and I will. Give me Supernatural Foresight about people, places, my own destiny and other people's purposes. Give me a sixth sense that lets me know when even perfect strangers need me. Show me what they need and how best to give it to them. Grant me the insight to know the difference between my own selfish desires (and even my well-meaning ones) and Your will for my life. Make me a fast learner who won't need to hear things more than once for it to stick or for me to obey and take action. Let me be like fertile soil that soaks up all the knowledge it can get. Let me know when a trial is a trial that I should push through versus a roadblock You've personally put in my way to stop me from going down the wrong path. Let me see the "green" in profitable opportunities so that I know when to sign on and let me see flashing red stop lights when I should be running the other way. Help me to have x-ray vision that sees straight through people right to their heart and their intentions. Let me instantly discern good from evil. Help me to know when people mean well and will do right by me. Especially, let me know right away when they mean me harm. Give me an alarm that tells me I should jump into a conversation and stand up for You and what is right. Give me another one that lets me know I'd be casting my pearls before swine and wasting my time. I'm asking for Your righteous wisdom to be implanted in me. In Your Holy Name, Amen.

Are there any situations that currently have you confounded? Maybe there are some people you just can't figure out. Maybe there's a distraction masquerading as an opportunity and you need His guidance in deciphering it all. List those issues here and ask Him boldly for this dynamic gift of discernment. Watch closely as He begins to reveal powerful subtleties about people and situations that will provide life-changing clarity. Then, be sure to act on that inside information.

_____

_____

_____

_____

_____

_____

_____

_____

_____

_____

_____

_____

_____

_____

_____

Day 4: A Prayer to Keep Away the Riff Raff

1 Corinthians 15:33 (NIV)

Do not be misled: "Bad company corrupts good character."

Deuteronomy 1:13 (NIV)

Choose some wise, understanding and respected men from each of your tribes, and I will set them over you."

When you've got big business plans that involve fulfilling your destiny you can start off by yourself, but eventually you're going to need a team. In one fell swoop, that team can give you wings or sink you like the Titanic. You'll need to choose wisely.

Lord, my time is precious because You gave it to me as a gift, a new gift each day. I know I am not entitled to it. Help it not to be wasted by others who don't mean me well. Keep away from me people who behave like energy vampires and mood downers. Keep away complainers who might suck me into their hopelessness and doubters who want me to share in their fear. Clear my path of jealous people and naysayers and don't allow me to operate in that way towards others. Also keep away carrot danglers who are all talk and no results. Keep me away from status quo huggers and easily satisfied people who have settled for mediocrity. Only allow me to pair myself with team members who share my passion, my work ethic and my idea of success that should ultimately be Your idea of success. Surround me with people who are smarter than me, people that I can learn from. Put me in the midst of people who also need my counsel, then give me the words to say. Let me speak Your sage advice to them instead of my own opinions. Mostly, hide me from bringers of chaos and emotional wrecks not yet ready to help me or to be helped. Cause me to spend my time and energy on people who need me and can most take advantage of the help I have to give. Cause me to surround myself with people who are wise beyond their years and have invaluable lessons to share. Put me in the company of the people for which You have intended me to interact. I trust my future world changing team to You, in Your holy name, Amen.

This is a hard one. Make a list of the riff raff in your life. You know who they are, but you've been pretending that being with them, hanging around them, partying with them, dating them, taking their advice, or endlessly giving them advice they never take is not really doing you all that much harm. But deep down you know better. Pray over them. Ask God to help them in ways that you never could so you can be released from them and free to do His work.

_____

_____

_____

_____

_____

_____

_____

Now list the wise people in your life, your mentors or those from whom you'd like to learn more and glean more. Pray over them. Ask God to more firmly insert them in your life. Ask Him as well to bless them for how they have so selflessly poured into you thus far.

_____

_____

_____

_____

_____

Day 5: A Prayer for Crystalline Clarity and Fueled Focus

Proverbs 19:21 (NIV)

Many are the plans in a person's heart, but it is the LORD's purpose that prevails.

If you're anything close to brilliant (and you know you are), people have either called you "all over the place" or contrastingly "tunnel-visioned". If you're all over the place, you're likely multitalented and have ideas overflowing at the speed of light. That's great, but you'll need even more focus than most to be sure all of the best of your ideas see the light of day. More importantly, you'll want to be sure you're walking in your purpose. Not all great ideas lead to purpose and that's the path you need to stay on. If you're admittedly tunnel-visioned, you've probably tuned in to the fact that you're created for a very specific purpose and you're intent on not dropping the ball. But you have a tendency not to see important things happening around you that could put you on a faster track to getting where you're ultimately supposed to be. Clarity and Focus will be equally important for you no matter which category you fall into.

God, with the many talents You have gifted me, You know more than anyone that I can become distracted. I have so many irons in the fire I need You to tell me when which one should get the most heat. Help me to keep my new ideas coming, but show me how to keep them organized and prioritized by which one You most want me to complete right away. Let me know which one I'm most capable of completing utilizing the strengths I have right now. Clue me in to which one will bring the most profit emotionally, spiritually and financially, and which one is most relevant right now. Don't let me be fooled into jumping from one project that is underway for one that is shiny and new. Still yet, give me flexibility in my focus so that I can serve You in the moment. Help me to discern between true opportunity and rootless distraction. Help me to tell the difference between a good deal and a worthy project from a half-baked hope. In the process, don't let me be deterred by doubt that my idea is too lofty because I know You gave me grand vision. When I look at my past, I've rarely done things on a small scale and I know in my heart that's how You have wired me. Don't let me be discouraged by focusing on what I don't currently have in my arsenal or in my personal stash of contacts and resources, because I know You wouldn't give me these grand visions without the means to accomplish them. Strengthen my strengths and help me develop my weaknesses into strengths. As much as I want to help others, do not let me distract myself by putting off my own projects to help someone who has not even truly begun to focus fully on the thing they are asking me to help them with. I know that sometimes my own destiny is at risk when I put it off to help someone reach his or hers. Help me to remember I'm most useful and most able to lift others up when I'm operating in the mode and at the level of where You need me to be. In Your Holy Name, Amen.

You can admit it. Are you a fellow shaken bottle of soda pop, meaning you have a gazillion ideas bubbling over at any given moment? That's not a bad thing and don't let anyone tell you otherwise. It is a blessing to be multi-gifted! But you'll need to focus that fizz and He can do that for you. List your many ideas here and begin to pray that He begins to clearly highlight the one you should lead with. Ask Him to help you prioritize them based on profit in all the ways listed in the prayer. Once the priority emerges ask Him for Supernatural Focus to get you zooming and being more productive than you've ever been.

_____
_____
_____
_____
_____
_____
_____
_____
_____
_____
_____
_____
_____
_____

Tunnel-visioned are we? List your current obsession(s) here. Ask God to widen your gaze just enough so you can see the help He is placing in your midst. Allow Him to help you balance important aspects like your family and friends who you know you can sometimes ignore when you're in the zone. He can show you when they need you most and He can show you how to plug them in so they don't feel left out of your destiny.

_____

_____

_____

_____

_____

_____

_____

_____

_____

_____

_____

_____

_____

_____

_____

Day 6: A Prayer for the Gift of Transformative Leadership

Exodus 18:25 (NIV)

He chose capable men from all Israel and made them leaders of the people, officials over thousands, hundreds, fifties and tens.

More than likely, if you felt led to read this type of a devotional, you're going to be or always have been called on to lead. And while you were probably Student Body President, captain of your sports team, pastor, CEO or all of the above, even natural born leaders need divine guidance, mostly to be sure we get out of our own way.

Lord, help me to understand the difference between leading and simply bossing people around. Teach me how to respect and treat my followers, especially my first followers, like the equals they are. I want to be a leader at the forefront in terms of strategy, execution and innovation so please empower me with the skills needed to make that a reality. Make me unafraid to step out into the unknown, to try something untested. Give me a knack for hiring brilliant minds and don't allow me to be intimidated by those that are smarter than me, they will be invaluable to my future. Teach me to speak in a way that provides clarity and not confusion. Warn me against favoritism and nepotism so that the most qualified and the most talented or simply the people who have something special to bring to the table get into the right spots. Don't allow me to get offended when my leadership is questioned, especially if it needs to be questioned. Make me the kind of leader that inspires a team to be at their best and to operate at world changing levels. Make me a groomer of future extraordinary leaders who will go out and change the world through their calling. Don't allow me to be offended when it's time for them to leave my nest and make it on their own. Show me how to give second chances without handicapping my operation, but also give me the guts to cut ties when need be. Make my words edifying and not condescending or insulting and make me the kind of authority people revere instead of fear. At the same time, train me to be formidable and to carry myself in a way that garners a warm, thorough respect. Help me practice what I preach so that no one can ever call me a hypocrite. Don't let me be double minded or unstable. Give me ideas and give me a sixth sense about who to share them with and who to ask for help. Help me to be a friendly leader without feeling the need to be everybody's friend. But show me when to make myself available to someone in need on my team. Help me to care about what's right ahead of what's popular. Give me the power to make and execute tough decisions. Give me the warrior smarts of David and his ever-dependence on Your guidance. Lead me into all of my battles. Make me wise like Solomon and let me inherit his gift of growing wealth. Make me fearless and multifaceted like Deborah and show me when to jump in when needed. I'm praying for fearless, thoughtful, revolutionary leadership that only comes from You. Amen.

Are you a leader? Or do you want to lead? Why do you want to lead? Who or what do you see yourself leading? Maybe you're afraid of leadership or don't trust people to follow correctly? Whether you have the guts to lead or not doesn't really matter. Ask Moses, or Saul for that matter! If you're destined to lead, you'll be thrust into a leadership position soon, so ask God in advance to prepare you and to position you how He sees fit. Consider what you want your leadership brand to look and feel like and ask God to turn you into the leader He destined you to become.

_____

_____

_____

_____

_____

_____

_____

_____

_____

_____

_____

_____

_____

_____

Day 7: A Prayer for the Gift of Preparation

Ezekiel 38:7 (NIV)

"'Get ready; be prepared, you and all the hordes gathered about you, and take command of them.

2 Timothy 4:2 (NIV)

Preach the word; be prepared in season and out of season; correct, rebuke and encourage—with great patience and careful instruction.

Here's the thing. Winging it is a great skill to have. It's wonderful to have spontaneity and the talent of "pulling it off" at your disposal. But it should only be a back-pocket skill you use when need be, it shouldn't be your mode of operation. Cold, hard, spirit-led preparation should be your routine.

Father God, do not let me forsake my God-given talents by not doing any earthly practice, earthly research and preparation. Make me a good steward of my gifts and never let me take them for granted. Remind me that "winging it" is a skill to be utilized only when necessary. Help me not to ever use it as a default mode of operation. Just because something comes easily to me, don't let me slip into complacency and ill preparedness. Make me care deeply about how effective I am and warn me when I am functioning below potential. Give me a love for getting ready, a desire for order, organization and thoroughness. Don't let me coast on the leftover diesel fumes of my last brilliant performance. Teach me how to over prepare and train like a world-class athlete so that I'm ready for almost anything and can adapt easily to my surroundings. Help me avoid falling into laziness, procrastination or the habit of making excuses for subpar performances. Give me the strength, energy and focus to be in top-notch condition whenever I'm called on for duty. And then after all of that readiness, remind me to leave room for You to step in and work Your magic, be it the middle of my presentation or in my business plan or in the third lap of a four-lap mile. Then, let me be prepared to let You take over. I understand the power of Your anointing and I know that it is greatly increased when applied to my thorough preparation, because then You can come in and work through me instead of in spite of me. Prepare me for that Heavenly Father, Amen.

Are you a preparer or a procrastinator? It's really that simple. Procrastination doesn't even have to be the kiss of death IF you learn the art of preparing in crunch time. Some of us thrive on a good deadline and that's ok, but we mustn't forget why we need time for preparation. It's actually the time when God speaks to us and gives us intel on what's up ahead. If you're always in frantic mode, you might slip up and be awesome, but He wants to make your awesomeness a guarantee every time. Turn to Him in time to let Him work. List your preparation tendencies and how you want God to reform them. Then watch yourself develop a zeal for getting ready!

Day 8: A Prayer for Supernatural Handsomeness & Ravishing Beauty

1 Samuel 16:12 (NIV)

So he sent for him (David) and had him brought in. He was glowing with health and had a fine appearance and handsome features. Then the LORD said, "Rise and anoint him; this is the one."

Studies show pretty people have it best. They get unfair advantage, unfair favor, and unfair consideration. But you don't have to worry about being objectified or overlooked because your gift will speak for itself when God is backing you. You can rest assured that even if your beauty gets you a second look, you'll be more than qualified for the job. So asking for a little supernatural help in the good looks department can only help matters. You can also be confident that even if, in the natural, you don't look like the people in fashion magazines, God's supernatural makeover will make you radiant AND make room for you at any table.

Lord, I may or may not be the best-looking person in the room but I want You to make it so anyway. I ask this not out of vanity, but because I understand I'm Your representative and that's a big deal. Help me first to see myself as beautifully and wonderfully made. But also make other people see me as impossibly gorgeous, magnetic and irresistible. Make my blemishes appear to be beauty marks. Make it so people think my bad hair days are style trends. Give me a sense of style that will speak to whomever my ideal audience might be. Guide my choices so that they are both stunning and appropriate. Make heads turn so that I can then throw the attention on You. Make it so my face glows and even my overbite has charm. Make the sound of my voice endearing even if it's a bit raspy. Transform me into something that simply looks like a ray of light. The light will be so bright people won't even really be seeing me, but they'll be seeing You. People will see me and they'll smile, they'll hear me laugh and they'll find joy enough to laugh with me. The beauty You give me will transcend the kind found in a Victoria's Secret catalog or a muscle magazine cover because it will come with Supernatural Substance. I'll be more handsome than I really am in real life because You'll make it so in the eyes of those staring my way. When people take that second look, when I'm being unknowingly appraised for opportunity, have them look at me and say, "This is the one." In the natural, help me to care for my own appearance. Break me out of lazy habits that don't do my first impression justice. Help me not to squander the natural beauty You've given me. As beautiful as You make me, keep me humble in all of my ravishing gorgeousness. I dare to ask even this in Your Holy Name, Amen.

Remind yourself of the physical attributes that people have told you make you beautiful. List as well the things you love about yourself in terms of inner AND outer beauty. Thank God for those aspects of yourself.

_____

_____

_____

_____

_____

Now, list the physical insecurities you have and be honest about how your self-consciousness about those things has secretly held you back. Ask God to make them non-factors, to restore your confidence and show you how those little imperfections have no bearing on your success in Him.

_____

_____

_____

_____

_____

_____

_____

Finally, be candid about the areas you know you need to work on. Whether you need to be bolstered in the area of be self-control, discipline or self-motivation in order to achieve your physical best or maybe your not-so-awesome attitude takes away from your beauty. Ask Him to strengthen those areas and give you the desire to make necessary changes.

_____

_____

_____

_____

_____

_____

_____

_____

_____

_____

_____

_____

_____

_____

_____

_____

_____

Day 9: A Prayer for Unfair Favor

Esther 2:15 (NIV)

When the turn came for Esther (the young woman Mordecai had adopted, the daughter of his uncle Abihail) to go to the king, she asked for nothing other than what Hegai, the king's eunuch who was in charge of the harem, suggested. And Esther won the favor of everyone who saw her.

Some people say you need a little bit of talent and a whole lotta luck to be incredibly successful in this life. I replace the word "luck" with "favor". What I'm realizing in looking over my own life and the lives of people who are where I want to be is that we all have received favor and many times the favor was unwarranted. In other words, when you look with natural eyes, someone may have been more qualified or was waiting longer or seemingly deserved something more than you. You might have seen this happen in your own life. It might have even made you uncomfortable. Nevertheless…it was you who got the opportunity. To be clear, the favor I'm talking about is not the kind bestowed on us by man, like the luck of being let into the good 'ol boys club or the cool girl clique. It's not even something we get for being incredibly good, talented and well behaved. The favor I'm referring to is a gift of grace from God Himself. He gives it to us for His own purposes to be fulfilled more than for us simply to get stuff we want. Favor often comes in the form of extreme talents and giftedness in areas where there is a dearth or extreme financial blessings that come from what looks to be a Midas touch or extreme access to places we have no business being in, or at least we could not have gotten there by our own devices. You will need God's high favor to get behind doors that are usually locked to others who desperately want to get in.

Father God, I know I'm smart, talented and even sort of good looking. I've got impressive connections and my own significant resources that I've built up over time. I'm a hard worker, extremely competitive and can get a lot done by myself. But now I want You to take over. I'm at the end of the DIY road and in order to get to the ultimate Level Next, I need Your favor. I need the kind of high favor that grants me access to important ears and then the kind of high favor that gives me the right words to speak into them. I need the high favor that bulldozes doors others are patiently knocking on. I need the kind of unfair favor that takes me to the front of the line, puts my application on top of the pile, allows me to get the last bit of funding available for my project or the last meeting on the schedule of that important person You want me to meet. But don't let me confuse Your unfair favor as a pass to act unfairly towards others. Let me be mindful that I'm in my new position *because* of Your grace and that I need to treat the people around me graciously. Keep me mindful of the fact that just because I've received unfair favor, it doesn't make me better than anyone. It just simply means I was created for "such a time as this" and if I'm being divinely pushed to the front of the line, I have even more responsibility to get the job done now, sooner rather than later. Grant me Your high favor in order to operate favorably, oh Heavenly Father, Amen.

What, to whom, and to where do you still need access? Only list gates that would be impossible for you to get beyond without God's intervention on your behalf. Think big. Then believe that He is the Ultimate Gatekeeper and He holds the skeleton key to any door you need to walk through to access your destiny and fulfill His will.

_____

_____

_____

_____

_____

_____

_____

_____

_____

_____

_____

_____

_____

_____

_____

Day 10: A Prayer for Mother Teresa-like Compassion

Philippians 2:3-4 (NIV)

Do nothing out of selfish ambition or vain conceit. Rather, in humility value others above yourselves, not looking to your own interests but each of you to the interests of the others.

1 Peter 4:10 (NIV)

Each of you should use whatever gift you have received to serve others, as faithful stewards of God's grace in its various forms.

In all our getting and conquering, we must be balanced by way of making an impact on this earth that does more than increase our bank accounts or bring us recognition. Our presence should radiate warmth even if we're cold-hard competitors. A true hero can be measured by the percentages represented in their life. A large part of that percentage should be devoted to sacrifice. Sacrifices of time, energy, money and love devoted towards others should make up a great percentage of the pie graph that is our life. Especially for driven people, God will have to grant you the space in your heart and mind to make room for others and not just your ambitions, no matter how worthy.

God, do not let me leave this earth with a legacy that doesn't involve positively and selflessly impacting the lives of others. Help me to give without my first thought being about the tax break I'm going to receive. Help me to spend time helping others when I know up front there will be no tangible return, recognition or emotional kickback other than the knowledge that I'm participating in changing a life. Give me eyes to see the right opportunities in which to become involved. Let strangers see areas in which I can help them and give them the courage to ask me for my help. On the other hand, don't let me get involved in causes just because I feel obligated, but not supernaturally drawn to. I know that will only result in me feeling miserable and also cause the organization to resent my half-hearted involvement. Make my efforts to help people inspire others to help as well. Tell me how big to write my checks, make me generous in everything from tipping restaurant servers to being a significant part of groundbreaking ceremonies for powerful organizations doing powerful things for powerless people because I understand my calling is to be a blessing. Give me the means to be an underwriter, a platinum level sponsor, a patron of worthy causes run by people who know how to run them. Let me give without asking for my name on the building. Maybe it's my brain they'll need, give me the ideas to help propel other people's missions as well as my own. Give me an open heart capable of empathizing, understanding, sympathizing, loving, and cherishing beyond compare. Let people feel the depths of my compassion for them and let it be healing for them, healing that revives and rejuvenates. In all of this help me to remain humble when I see the fruits of my giving. Keep my heart pure, in Your Holy Benevolent Name, Amen.

What are the causes or the issues or the people you have the greatest compassion for? What group of people, what behavior, what issues have you NOT developed a sensitivity towards that you know deep down you should examine? Ask God to bolster your empathy, to make you an effective advocate for organizations you love and to turn your heart towards issues or people you haven't shown much mercy for in the past. To be the effective world changer you're designed to be, He'll need you at your least judgmental and your most compassionate.

_____

_____

_____

_____

_____

_____

_____

_____

_____

_____

_____

_____

_____

_____

_____

Day 11: A Prayer for the Power to Forgive Others Unreasonably

Colossians 3:13 (NIV)

Bear with each other and forgive one another if any of you has a grievance against someone. Forgive as the Lord forgave you.

In the course of going after what you're meant to have and who you're meant to be, you are going to get screwed over a few times. That boyfriend or girlfriend is going to dump you right when things are beginning to take off, or worse yet, when things are seemingly crumbling all around you they'll desert you. That husband or wife is going to all of a sudden make unreasonable demands or lose faith in you and it's going to feel like a wet blanket thrown on your inner fire. Even with all this audacious prayer someone is still going to double cross you or hurt you. That's not negative talk. It's reality. You're going to have to deal with that and then... you're going to have to forgive them.

Jesus, Jesus, Jesus! Help me to develop a heart now that knows how to forgive so it will come as second nature when I really won't want to "let it go". Help me not waste space in my being by cluttering my inner self with grudges and plans for revenge. Don't find me spending

43

my whole life plotting the destruction of those who've hurt my loved ones and me. I'm going to need You to help me know when to walk away and when to seek Your guidance concerning taking legal action. I'm asking You to personally heal my wounds so I won't begin to replace them with dangerously self-destructive habits. When people wrong me, let me know when it's not my fault and make it equally clear when I've brought it on myself. Help me understand people's motives when they betray me. Teach me a lesson from it that I won't forget, help me to see that same type of person coming my way in the future so that I can stop them dead in their tracks. Better yet, You block them for me. In love, don't let me allow a bad previous experience from the past to keep me from my soul mate in the future. But also don't let a bad month with my mate make me give up on something worth cherishing. Still yet, teach me how to both forgive and still walk away from a bad relationship or partnership simultaneously. Help me see the difference between a perceived wrong and a real one so that I won't be carrying around unnecessary negativity towards someone who truly meant me no harm. Don't let past wrongs done to me shape my mode of operation when it comes to how warmly I treat new people I meet in personal and business relationships. Father, the hardest thing in the world for me to do is to forgive myself. Sometimes it's just easier to beat myself up instead so I'm asking You not to allow me to pummel myself, also a child of God. Help me to forgive like You do almost to the point of forgetting, but remembering just enough to keep me safely moving forward without repeating my mistakes. Lord, I know in my heart I will need You to help me with this...big time. In Your Holy Name I pray, Amen.

List who has hurt you. It's easier to list that than to ask you, "Who do you need to forgive?" Either way, it's the same list. Make sure your name is on it. Now ask God to make it possible.

_____

_____

_____

_____

_____

_____

_____

_____

_____

_____

_____

_____

_____

_____

_____

_____

_____

_____

Day 12: A Prayer for the Power to Ask and Accept Help

Isaiah 41:13 (NIV)

For I am the LORD your God who takes hold of your right hand and says to you, Do not fear; I will help you.

Psalm 20:2 (NIV)

May he send you help from the sanctuary and grant you support from Zion.

As a DIY'er (Do-it-yourself-er), you are used to and often most comfortable going it alone. There's a lot to be said for that independence, but in order to get where you truly need to be, in order to bump things up a notch, you are going to need the "H" word. Help. I use the word HELP countless times in these prayers because it's hard for people like us to ask for it. We must learn to ask for it. So I figured we should first be able to ask for help from The Helper Himself. But there will come a point where you'll need earthly help from people who know more than you, have more insight or resources than you, or more contacts and more experience. Here's the thing we often don't realize, people who can help you usually *want* to help you. They have a heart made to help in a certain area. I enjoy helping aspiring artists, so when they ask me for help they're usually overwhelmed by all the help I give them for free! But it's what I was created for, to offer that sort of assistance, so I feel relieved when I'm able to operate in that way. The key is asking the right people at the right time in the right way. And then we have to learn to be able to receive the help they are offering.

Father, You know it's hard for me to ask for help. It doesn't come naturally for me. But I'm asking You now to always show me when I'm at the end of my rope and need to look elsewhere for assistance. Help me be happy in asking and help me be gracious in receiving. Sometimes, people are going to offer unsolicited help. Help me know when I need what they're offering and make it so I never turn down good help out of pride or fear of looking helpless. Send me helpers who genuinely have a heart and the skill for what I'm working on and scan them for impure motives before they come my way. Don't let me perceive accepting help as a sign of weakness. Show me what kind of specific help to ask for and help me discern when, who and how to ask. Remind me that when I delay in asking for the help I need, I'm delaying Your work. Remind me that when I delay in asking for help, I'm needlessly depleting my own energy sources and I'm bringing exhaustion on myself. Go ahead and make me an expert in asking for help and searching for guidance and let it become easier for me each time I do it. When I'm able, help me bless my helper as they have blessed me. With all that is within me, I ask for Your help in this matter. Bless You, Father God, Amen.

What do you need help with right now? List the smallest things to the greatest. Nothing is to small or too big to be assisted. But if you don't ask, no one will know you need help in the area in which they are so capable of giving. Ask now and watch God send you the perfect helpers for your situation.

_____

_____

_____

_____

_____

_____

_____

_____

_____

_____

_____

_____

_____

_____

_____

_____

_____

_____

Day 13: A Prayer to Be Able to Receive Recognition

Exodus 9:16 (NIV)

But I have raised you up for this very purpose, that I might show you my power and that my name might be proclaimed in all the earth.

It sounds incompatible, but even super humans often shy away from recognition. Those of us that really understand the way God works know that our powers are not our own. So when we do something great, we understand it's Him doing something great through us. Because of this knowledge, it is sometimes uncomfortable for us to receive what often feels like undue recognition. But even in the Bible, God puts an emphasis on being recognized. It's something He promised to many of the great figures in the Bible. He often made a promise of making their name great even when they weren't looking for greatness and recognition. God knows you aren't perfect so you don't need to point that out to Him and everybody that tries to recognize you. When you sit back and look at it, you're being used as an important vessel. Many times knowing the person behind the great achievement is what draws more people in. It allows you the opportunity not just to accept a plaque, but also to tell your story. Recognition of you will often be recognition of God's grace, power, mercy and favor. Don't deny Him that opportunity.

Father, while You keep me humble don't let me miss out on an opportunity to be recognized and to honor You in the process. Help me get comfortable accepting praise because You've warned me lots more of it is coming my way in this season. Make me stand still and receive the applause You're showering on me at this point of my life. Don't let me turn away in undue shame. But never let me forget that what is really being praised is Your grace and Your greatness. Help me welcome recognition as a chance to tell the truth behind my successes. Help me dispel the myth of man's greatness by using the moment for Your glory. While I need You to help me receive recognition, be sure my focus never becomes to seek it. Let me be absolutely fine without it, but help me to make the most of it when it does come my way. In the times where I know in my heart that the real recognition is due someone else, help me redirect the spotlight and learn to wait my turn. My day will come; in fact it comes every day because of You. I ask for this quality with full expectance in Your Holy name, Amen.

Are there certain times or situations where you find it difficult to accept recognition? Maybe you feel under recognized? In what areas? List them below. Either way God can simultaneously help you learn how to be satisfied by working in excellence with Him without seeking recognition. He'll also show you how to graciously accept it when it finds you.

_____

_____

_____

_____

_____

_____

_____

_____

_____

_____

_____

_____

_____

_____

_____

_____

_____

Day 14: A Prayer for the Power to Accept 180's

Isaiah 55:8-9 (NIV)

"For my thoughts are not your thoughts, neither are your ways my ways," declares the LORD. "As the heavens are higher than the earth, so are my ways higher than your ways and my thoughts than your thoughts."

Highly successful people have either been doing things the same way for a long time or they're always looking to improve and adapt. Healthy status quo or not, since God is not a stagnant God, He will usually require us to change at some point and often it's right when we're finally getting settled into where we are. I believe God hates complacency and you should, too.

God, You know I like things my way. I've got a routine that's worked well for me and I've got a good thing going. I've got a perfect plan in my head of how things should play out when it comes to my life. That's why it's hard for me to accept that You might want me to start doing things differently or worse yet, change my course altogether. Let me know how to tell the difference between a rut and a routine that consistently and constantly bears new fruit. Prepare my heart now to be able to receive fast-approaching change, because even though I know You're a God of consistency, You're also a God of transition and next level elevation. You know I can be stubborn and sometimes tend to lean on my own understanding so I ask You to remind me instantly of how much higher Your ways are to mine. Pry old childhood dreams out of my hands and exchange them with grown up destinies! Help me to remember You'd never move me backwards so even though change might be scary, when You're the orchestrater, I can trust it's going to be good for me. Alert me to The Shift, where You begin to politely close old doors that represent me wrongly trying to go back to doing business as usual. You'll begin to blow open new doors that will unexpectedly allow me to operate in gifts that have been underutilized or hidden up until now. Maybe I've been running from this new season, secretly afraid of the bigness of it. Remind me I'm built to handle this era You're taking me into. Help me shed old skin. Make foreign concepts familiar, give me new languages quickly, put new tastes in my mouth, make me as adaptable as a chameleon in new environments. Father, if a 180 is in my future, stretch my mental muscles to be able to be ready for it and even to rejoice in it when it comes. Give me new eyes to recognize the seasons for change. Give me new feet to be able to jump right into them fearlessly. Let Your will always be done over my own, always. Amen.

Have you been noticing you've been getting nudged or not so gently turned in a new direction? Make note of these shifts in attention, desire and focus. Notice how things you once loved are starting to lose a bit of their flavor and then ask God to show you what He wants you to develop a new taste for instead. Also list what scares you most about these big changes and ask for His peace and guidance in those areas. Watch Him make the transition smoother than you ever imagined.

_____

_____

_____

_____

_____

_____

_____

_____

_____

_____

_____

_____

_____

_____

_____

_____

_____

_____

Day 15: A Prayer for the Quick Silver Ability to Surrender

Proverbs 16:3 (NIV)

Commit to the LORD whatever you do, and he will establish your plans.

Our plans are pretty awesome, especially when you ask us. So it's hard to imagine that everything you dream might not be what you're supposed to be manifesting right now. Usually there's a glimpse of your destiny revealed in your desires and dreams but more often than not, if we haven't been spending time asking God exactly what to ask for, we've probably missed the mark a bit in terms of what it is we're supposed to have and what we're supposed to do. So we'll need to know how to dream big, put things into action and...surrender the outcome.

Father God, help me to give legs to the dreams You give me without painting my own limited image of what I think the outcome will look like exactly. I know that if I hold on stubbornly enough to my vision of my dream, You'll eventually just let me have my wimpy version and I DON'T want that! Instead, help me keep a firm determination but also a loose grip so that I can grab on to Your version of Your dream for me instead. I'm surrendering my plans, my desires, my dreams, my suggestions, my intentions, my schemes and especially my will to You. I'm determined not to want anything more than I want You and Your will for my life. In fact, I surrender my life to You, my education, my family, my career are all in Your capable hands. When I start wanting You more than anything it makes surrendering everything else that much easier. When it comes to my destiny I refuse to operate like a control freak because I understand having You in control will bring the best outcomes possible. Help me to accept that my eyes, my ways and my thoughts are not Yours, so I might not always understand some of Your maneuvers. Keep me from operating in manipulation to get my way. Cleanse me of ulterior motives. Ward off frustration when I've been pleading with You without getting the answer I thought I wanted. Don't let me be angry with You and turn against You because of it. Grant me patience to wait on Your will that I know You will reveal to me in Your time. Teach me how to pray so I can start to sense what it is that I should desire. Remind me that when I know what to ask for, I'll start getting more yes's from You. That's when I'll start asking followed by receiving. That's when I'll knock, and doors will be opened. God, I'm seriously asking You to take control. I mean it for real this time. For real. Amen.

List the things you have the toughest time surrendering? Surrendering is about trusting God so don't get so caught up worrying about trusting things to people. Pray over this list and ask God to give you the power to begin to relinquish these things into His care.

_____

_____

_____

_____

_____

_____

_____

_____

_____

_____

_____

_____

_____

_____

_____

_____

_____

_____

_____

Day 16: A Prayer for Powerful Eloquence and Persuasion in Speech

Exodus 4:12 (NIV)

Now go; I will help you speak and will teach you what to say."

Ephesians 4:29 (NIV)

Do not let any unwholesome talk come out of your mouths, but only what is helpful for building others up according to their needs, that it may benefit those who listen.

The power of the mighty word, especially when spoken eloquently, intelligently and passionately has the ability to change mindsets, laws and modes of operation. Great influence is needed to effect great world change and great ideas have to be communicated effectively in order to get the ball rolling. Even if you've gotten by on not saying much, when you do speak your words need to be heard, they need to have staying power to stick on the minds of those who hear you, transformative power to change the hearts of those listening, and activating power to cause others not just to listen but to move. Paul was noted for having this gift. Every time he opened his mouth "many were added" to the faith. He also had a gift for debate and argument that he learned to use and curb at will. You'll want to exercise this discretion as well.

Father, I believe that out in the world are sets of ears specifically tuned to the exact frequency of my voice. So help me embrace any opportunity to speak to groups both big and small so that I find myself whispering into the ears of my ideal audience, the ones You've created me to provide solutions for. Clear the heads of the audience members so they have space to receive what it is I'm sharing with them and stirring within them. Help me conquer any fear I might have about looking or sounding foolish and replace it with the confidence of knowing I'm able to move the masses with my voice. Let the sound of my voice resonate deeply with those who hear it. Let it be like a flood that awakens dormant areas and creates an unforgettable, uncomfortable friction that forbids people to stay where they've been for way too long. Let me be able to reverse decisions that You're against, let me change minds and outcomes that You want redirected. Still yet, I don't want to revert to performing in my own brilliance. Instead let me reflect You, let them hear You when I speak. Give me the perfect words for the thoughts I'm trying to communicate, help me paint pictures in the minds of the listening audience, help me put phrases together in a way that heals wounds and inspires people to action. Even if I'm normally not so exciting, make my presentations inspirational, motivational, informative and entertaining. Train me to open and close effectively, purposefully, powerfully and memorably. Don't let my words fall on deaf ears, Father, let people hear what I'm saying; let my sage advice fall on fertile soil. Help my speeches gain in momentum and effectiveness as each minute passes. Help me change things up on the spot depending on whom I'm speaking to. I don't want to be afraid to veer off of the script if I sense the audience needs something other than what I've prepared. Better yet, let me get to a point where I don't even need a script because I will begin to allow You to give me the exact words in the exact moment. Let me use examples and tell stories that make people feel like I'm talking directly to them, speaking directly into their lives. But stop me from chasing rabbits that won't bear fruit. Don't let me talk to hear myself talk, don't let me mindlessly talk about myself without a point to make. Let me know when I've gotten the audience in the palm of my hand so that at that exact moment I can impart exactly what it is You've sent me there for, and I can know that it will be received. Days, months, years after I've left the room, let Your essence stick on the walls, let my words ring true in the ears of those who heard me speak. For as long as need be, let whatever gift I've shared, whatever proverb I've told, whatever instructions I've given continue to bear fruit in the lives of the people who were there to hear it. Make me effective. Humbly, I ask for this supernatural power in Your Great Name, Amen.

Do you have fears surrounding public speaking? If so, list them and ask God to give you the confidence to overcome these fears. Then look for chances to speak in public and watch God begin to assuage your fears with each new opportunity.

_____

_____

_____

_____

_____

_____

If you're a confident speaker, list your not so helpful habits like chasing fruitless rabbits, rushing through important moments, showing off instead of leaving God room to show out, concluding mindlessly, etc. There's always room for improvement. Ask Him to strengthen your weak spots for an even more life-changing delivery.

_____

_____

_____

_____

_____

_____

_____

_____

Day 17: A Prayer for Heightened Listening

Proverbs 1:5 (NIV)

Let the wise listen and add to their learning, and let the discerning get guidance.

You're probably a great talker, but how are your listening skills? Believe it or not, your ability to listen acutely will be even more important than your ability to speak powerfully. Just as we expect God to listen keenly to us, we should do the same for others.

Lord, I'm asking You for heightened hearing. When people speak let me hear what they're *really* saying, what they're *really* asking for, what they're *really* needing. Help me listen in peace so that my mind is still and not turning over a hundred different thoughts while someone is thinking they're getting my attention. Let me hear between the sentences so that I come to know the true needs of a person even when they might not sense they're not telling me the whole story. Give me the insight to hear what's being said in the silences, the compassion to know when someone needs my help. Let me begin to listen to body language, read facial expressions and pick up on gestures. Let me hear what's really being communicated in sarcasm or disguised behind humor. Don't let me talk over people and interrupt them or make them feel their point of view is not valued. Make it so people know that if they want to truly be heard they can come to me. Let the word spread that I'm a great listener and then send the people who need to talk to me my way. From what I'm hearing, help me to devise the right plans and the best strategies. Never allow me to use what someone's telling me against them. Never allow me to spill confidences, especially under the guise of praying for or helping someone. More importantly, when someone is correcting me, let me be able to hear what they're saying without taking it personally. Let me know when they're right and let me discern when their issue is really with themselves. Show me how to respond in either situation. Finally, help me hear You! Let me listen early in the game so You don't have to lay me out or talk to me in the paralysis of tragedy. Let me listen BEFORE I have no other choice. Help me to hear You in others, in situations, in my inner voice, in my quiet time and in my gut-feelings. Replace my natural instinct with Your holy instinct. Give me ears as big as an elephant's. I'm asking You today for Supernatural Sonic Ability. I know that is not outside of the realms of Your possibility. In Your Jesus' Name I beg You for this one, Amen.

Do you feel like you can hear His voice clearly and undoubtedly? Or do you get confused on whether or not you're hearing your own inner voice or His? Ask Him to begin to make the distinction clearer and clearer. You'll first need to invest more time reading His word so you can learn His language and His ways. List the things you have difficulty hearing, literally, emotionally and spiritually and ask God to make you a heightened listener in those areas. As for people to people, what's your bad listening habit? He can help you fix that, too!

_____

_____

_____

_____

_____

_____

_____

_____

_____

_____

_____

_____

_____

_____

_____

_____

Day 18: A Prayer for a Grateful Spirit

Jonah 2:9 (NIV)

But I, with shouts of grateful praise, will sacrifice to you. What I have vowed I will make good. I will say, 'Salvation comes from the LORD.'"

Once you start getting more and more, you need to continually become more and more grateful. But you can start now even though you might not have everything you've dreamed of just yet. Remember that super humans usually are always looking for Level Next. That's a good thing and it's also the bane of our existence because contentment can be hard to come by if we're not careful to be grateful for what we have right NOW.

Thank You Father God for everything You've already given me. If You didn't grant one more wish or help me execute one more plan, I'd be more than eternally grateful for where I am today. I'm grateful for this day, for the people I'm blessed to have in my life right now, for the position I've been blessed to operate in up until this point. No amount of money, no new title, no new achievement will make me more grateful to You than I am right now because I know in my heart that even though I operate like a super human, in the end, I'm a mere mortal.

Although my hard work has been worthy of recognition, I know I'm no more deserving than the next person. I'm no more special, but for some reason You've granted me special powers that I'm grateful for. When I get restless about where I am, help me to remember where I started. When I get frustrated about what I don't have, peel the scales off of my eyes so I can see what surrounds me. When I get mad at the way the people in my life are acting, help me to imagine the despair I'd feel if they were no longer in my life. When I get stressed over having to choose between two really difficult options, help me to think about what it might be like to have no options. When I get tired of the journey, let me imagine my life with no purpose, without any path at all, let alone a difficult one. Maybe most miraculously, I should thank You for the things and people and tragedies You've saved me from without my knowing it. Thank You for the rejection that stung when it hit, but I can now see it was a form of divine protection. Thank You for the failures I'm able to repurpose. Thank You for the angels You send out before me and behind me that keep me and my loved ones safe. For Your grace that makes things way easier than they should be and for Your mercy that I don't even come close to deserving, I thank You wholeheartedly. Let me start my day in gratitude for simply waking up and taking another breath because that is more than many will have when each day breaks. Remind me constantly of what You've given me. Remind me it came without my earning or deserving it in the first place. You are Jehovah Jireh, Amen.

Sometimes my 7 year old son says, "You never let me do anything." I don't get angry anymore, I simply make him list the things we did for him that week alone. End of discussion. List the many, many things you have to be grateful for and let God know how grateful you are. Look at this list when you're feeling slighted by people or ignored by God and it will get you back on track. End of discussion.

_____

_____

_____

_____

_____

_____

_____

_____

_____

_____

_____

_____

_____

_____

_____

Day 19: A Prayer for a Healthy Domestic Life

Isaiah 32:18 (NIV)

My people will live in peaceful dwelling places, in secure homes, in undisturbed places of rest.

Because you are so darned focused on being larger than life, you will need God's help to be able to address the needs of your loving family that supports you and even your home that you've been blessed with. They need you, too. Do not resent them for doing so. You'll be so busy and on the move that your home will be especially important for serving as a place for recharging, refreshing, escape and peace.

Lord of my life, help me make sure my loved ones feel loved by me. Let my children feel cared for and protected enough so that they don't have to act out for my attention. Let them be balanced and capable of dealing with life's challenges. Let my spouse be eager to serve as my partner in life and let me be equally eager to serve them. Let food and drink be sweeter in our home than in the finest restaurants, let us enjoy each other's company more than we crave hanging out with friends. We will communicate well at every phase of life, even in tricky transitions. Help me to understand that the cleanliness of my surroundings affects my productivity. Let me clean the cobwebs of my household corners and the ones in my mind at the same time. Give me new air to breathe chock full of new possibilities as I dust and air out my natural surroundings. Let my nooks and crannies reflect the state of my affairs. Help me have nothing to hide at home or in my heart. Help me to balance my professional and my domestic life without resentment on either side. Help my spouse understand they need to chip in as well without turning me into a nag in the process. When I walk through the doors of my home from faraway places, let me bring blessings back with me. Let me instantly feel rest and peace when I cross my threshold. Since, I might be on the road more than at home, I'm asking You to dwell wherever I am.

Give my family understanding as I pursue my lofty purpose-based, destiny-oriented goals. Give them comfort in my absence, understanding in my dogged focus on things outside of the home. Keep them safe when I'm away. Do not let them hate my calling because they feel it takes me away from them. Assure them of my path so that they might walk with me and keep up with me with enthusiasm. Don't let them be reluctant about where I'm headed and where we're headed as a family. Let them be joyfully expectant with me. A healthy home and joyful family, I ask in Your name, Amen.

What are some areas in your household that you know you need to clean up before you're taken to the next level of responsibility? What things work well for your family? Ask God to preserve and strengthen those attributes.

Day 20: A Prayer for a Powerful Romantic Relationship

1 Corinthians 13:4-5 (NIV)

Love is patient, love is kind. It does not envy, it does not boast, it is not proud. It does not dishonor others, it is not self-seeking, it is not easily angered, it keeps no record of wrongs.

It's rare, but I do believe that some people have a destiny that never, ever involves having a personal romantic relationship with another person. From the Bible, Paul comes to mind. Think of nuns who spend their lives in love with and devoted to serving God through service and prayer. But for most of us, there is something called a soul mate outside of God. I don't believe we're supposed to look for them, but I do believe we find them in due time. You'll need God to put you in the right place at the right time in order to find your partner, the person who will love, support and be loyal to you. They'll also ground you and simultaneously uplift you. It's a rare person that can deal with your lofty dreams and your constant intensity, but they're out there waiting just for you. For those of you already in a powerful relationship, you'll need God to help you maintain it. Rest assured that the more successful you become, the more life changes will be required and the more retooling your relationship will need.

For the Unmarried: Ok God, here's what's up. I'm too busy to be out there looking for a spouse so I'm going to need You to check that box off for me! Speaking of boxes, I've got a long laundry list of requirements, ideals and physical specifications when it comes to my future mate. What I'm asking You to do is to help me forget that list. It's not that it's a bad list, but I'll need You to make sure I don't get so caught up in it that I miss the person You've destined for me. Help me know what points or areas I can afford to compromise on and which ones are sticking points that You created. Bring me a mate with like-minded beliefs, a similar code of ethics. Let us share likes and dislikes, political ideals, ideas on how to raise children and on familial roles. But don't be afraid to challenge me by way of my mate. I'll need someone who has the guts to tell me to, "Sit down, take a breath and listen!" They'll even not be afraid to tell me I'm (gulp)...wrong. They'll need to respect me, but not be afraid of my stature, my gifts or me. They should be able and secure enough to show genuine, over the top excitement for my successes and rejoice with me without getting too caught up in the hoopla themselves. I don't need a fan or a groupie. I need a partner. Let me be available enough to support them in their endeavors. Don't allow me to make our relationship all about me. Give me new eyes to see whether someone I'm involved with is dating me for me and not "Brand ME". Give them the strength to deal with my flaws in a loving manner. I can be a tough cookie, so give me the strength to be gentle, to dare to be vulnerable. While I'll want to find an equal that can hang with me and keep up with me, guide me to not be competing against them (unless it's video games or air hockey, etc.). I might need a companion that helps me in business, but don't let me marry for the sake of being a power couple. I might need a companion, who balances my intensity with serenity, let me recognize that. Send me a spouse that completes me to the point that I realize I never even knew I was missing something in my life before them. Their presence will change the way I view things, how I operate, how I treat people, even how I go about my business in a positive way. Thank You for being the Ultimate Matchmaker. You are the ultimate model of how we should love, help me to follow Your example. In Jesus' name, Amen.

What's on your list? See which ones match up with the ones God is telling you are on His list. Pray over those matches and ask Him to make the other stuff less important. You can always buy your new partner new shoes!

_____

_____

_____

_____

_____

_____

_____

_____

_____

_____

_____

_____

_____

_____

_____

_____

For the Married: Lord, strengthen what I have by way of this blessing You gave me as a soul mate. Help me to always see the goodness in their heart even when their actions don't always match. Help them to see the good in me when I'm not acting so wonderfully myself. Give me the desire to continually care about what makes them tick and what makes them happy. Never let me take this powerful partner of mine for granted. Help me want to stay attractive for them, but thank You that they won't hold my not-so-hot days against me. In fact, they'll love me more when I'm unglamorous. Help us to grow as our destinies unfold in front of us. Keep us in Your divine bubble of protection when Satan tries to come between us just as success hits. Let us bond stronger together in hard times and make it easy for us to rejoice authentically in each other's successes. In Your name, I bind up and put a restraining order on strife, confusion, chaos, resentment, unforgiveness, devastation, wayward thinking, pornographic interference, inappropriate relationships masquerading as "friendships". Mind my mouth when I speak about my spouse to my friends. Show me how to share with them without bashing my partner or belittling them. Help us share the spotlight if need be or allow one of us to be comfortable in the background if that's what the situation calls for. As a wife, I thank You for making my husband someone worthy of submitting to and continue to help him understand submission is not about servitude. As a husband, I praise You for giving me someone worthy of being put on a pedestal and cared for endlessly without allowing me to treat them like a trophy or objectify them. I know that You've called us to be together which means You've already equipped us to weather storms as a unit, to progress towards the highest levels of success as a team.

Keep us rolling on the floor laughing at each other, keep our inside jokes funny, continue to sharpen that silly language we share with only one another. Lastly, let my spouse realize what they have in me, let them value me and hold me in the highest esteem so that when I travel the world, no matter who flirts with me or tries to wine and dine me under the pretense of business, I'll remember what I have at home and that nothing can compare. I thank You for keeping me committed. In the Name of the Father of Sacred Unions, the Son, and the Holy Ghost, Amen.

List the strengths and potential weaknesses in your marriage. Pray fervently that God begin to help you be able to continue to rejoice in the strengths and to be honest about confronting the weak spots NOW. When the floodgates of elevation, success and anointing begin to flow, you want your relationship to withstand it and flourish in it. Ask Him to give you the timing and methodology to deal with those issues positively and conclusively.

_____

_____

_____

_____

_____

_____

_____

_____

_____

_____

_____

_____

_____

_____

_____

_____

_____

For those needing to get out of a poisonous relationship:

Father, I've been in this thing so long that even though I have an inkling of what I'm supposed to do, I'm having a hard time doing it. Give me the strength to see what the realities really are. Let me discern love from fearful dependence. Let me know the difference between weathering a common relational storm versus drowning in a cesspool of dysfunction. Let me recognize when my partner's words are not a salve, but a detriment to my soul. Help me keep track of whether or not I'm mostly miserable or mostly joyful in their presence. Especially, when we've already sought out guidance, help me to see that if I'm staying in a relationship where I'm suffering any kind of abuse at all, I'm only sabotaging my future and possibly even my life. Sometimes it's not going to be blatantly obvious because the infractions will seem minor on the surface, so I'm going to need You to simply point out when I'm in a relationship that's going no where fast. Remind me that an incompetent man will make an incompetent father. A shallow woman will make a shallow mother. In terms of my destiny, I ask You to free me of this distraction of a relationship, the one that's keeping me from advancing, from elevating. You know that I can't do the works You have planned for me while my hands are desperately clutching this raggedy baggage. Convict me if I'm constantly violating my own code of beliefs by staying in this relationship and forgive me for the compromises I've made thus far. But I declare that today is the day I begin the process of cutting all ties (physical, emotional, and psychological) with this person and begin to restore my soul to You so that You can restore my position and get me back on the road to fulfilling my purpose. I understand now that poisonous relationships are not matters of the heart, but matters of the soul and they interfere not just with our social lives, but also with our futures. I will listen when You lead me, Father. In Christ, I am kept. Amen.

People ALWAYS know when they're in a bad relationship. But let's say you're still in a state of denial. Make a list of Pros and Cons. Some cons we can learn to live with, like, "Always leaves the toilet seat up." Others we can't, like, "I never feel respected." Take a hard look at both sides of the list. When the cons greatly outweigh the Pros (even if it's just one awful Con), ask God to a). Show you the light and b). Show you the exit.

_____

_____

_____

_____

_____

_____

_____

_____

_____

_____

_____

_____

_____

_____

_____

Day 21: A Prayer to Ward off Inertia

Hebrews 6:11-12 (NIV)

We want each of you to show this same diligence to the very end, so that what you hope for may be fully realized. We do not want you to become lazy, but to imitate those who through faith and patience inherit what has been promised.

I've never wanted to quit. It's not in my DNA but I can admit that some days I feel stuck. I have been chugging along for so long, often not quite getting where I want to be and it makes me mad when I don't see the progress I've been counting on. When you hit that wall, you can get stalled, stuck in one place. You can also get used to being stuck and start to settle for staying where you are because it's actually easier than pushing through to the next level. During these periods, you and I will need Him to give us a boost. We'll need Him to jumpstart us, recharge us and redirect us.

Unglue my feet oh Lord, from the quagmire of failure, doubt, depression, procrastination and the incomprehensible fear of success. Do not let the dust of laziness or apathy settle over me. Help me to shake off setbacks and see possibility anew. Help me to transform failure into fresh instruction. Keep me away from people, situations, tv shows, websites, social media, music and food that waste my day, slow me down, sap my energy, or make me feel helpless. Guard my time ferociously and show me how to do the same. Give me the power of push through. Make forward movement a habit that I become addicted to. Make me a leaper and not a looker, a prayer and a doer. You are a God of action and since I am made in Your image, I am created and called to be action-packed. You are a God already in existence in my tomorrow and with gusto I will meet You there. I will finish what I start because You are a God of completion. I will not quit in the middle of my race. I will finish strong. I know, Father God, that if I am to see the fruition of the big vision You've given me, I cannot simple stand still but I must pray and execute Your word. Help me generate movement, stir up wind beneath my feet. If I get taken from this earth today, I will not be caught sitting in stagnancy. Don't let me hide behind the notion of waiting on You when You have already given me direction and a plan. Don't let the sun go down on my lack of accomplishment. Redirect an unfocused day into a powerful, purposeful one. I declare not one sunrise will find me slacking, not one sunset will question my existence. I will celebrate each week as follows: Momentum Mondays, Traction Tuesdays, Wisdom-filled Wednesdays, Thursdays will have Thrust behind them, Fridays will be Ferocious, Saturdays will have Savvy packed into them and my Sundays will be Spirit-filled, as will be all my days. I beg You to make me purposeful all of my days, every last one, even when I'm on vacation. Even when I am at rest and taking a much-needed break, I thank You that my past powerful actions will still be moving and working on my behalf. I know that in Your name it is possible that I will never be caught stuck, stalled and struggling again. Amen.

What's got you stuck? Indecision, doubt, depression, another person's delay, fear? Name it, call it out, tell it off and kick it out. List those roadblocks here and claim God's victory over each and every one of them.

_____

_____

_____

_____

_____

_____

_____

_____

_____

_____

_____

_____

_____

_____

_____

_____

_____

_____

_____

Day 22: A Prayer for the Ability to Embrace a New Day

Psalm 118:24 (KJV)

This is the day that the Lord hath made. I will rejoice and be glad in it.

Matthew 6:34 (NIV)

Therefore do not worry about tomorrow, for tomorrow will worry about itself. Each day has enough trouble of its own.

People like us spend so much time thinking about the far off future we forget how important and how *unpromised* each new day really is. We will need help to remember each day as a miracle rife with the possibility to reset, and a new opportunity to conquer new territory spiritually, professionally and personally.

God of this special day, I thank You for Your rare grace and mercy. I understand that the breath I just took was both a gift and a miracle in one. Around the world some people went to bed last night and didn't even wake up this morning. For some reason I wasn't one of them. I will take that reason to mean that You still have grand and important work for me to do on this earth. I know that even today is a part of my long-term destiny so I will not take it for granted in favor of tomorrow. So compel me to start this day and everyone after it in fellowship with You first. Time and time again You talk about how special the dawn hours are so in these morning moments, when I give You the first fruits of my time, I expect to receive my marching orders. Today, I will take steps towards my ultimate path. Today, I will make waves both big and small; I will be a catalyst for change in my own life as well as others. Even today, I'm a changed person and will not waste this day. People have cautiously reminded me that there is nothing new under the sun, but they have misunderstood You. I don't take that as a warning that there is nothing left to achieve or no more originality to be attained. I take it as a clue that I should look up above the stars to You for renewal and for originality instead of looking down here around me amongst mere men. Whether they worshipped You or not, You are the God of the greatest original thinkers of all time and since You are no respecter of persons, I take it to mean that I, too, am a revolutionary original thinker and in this New Day, I expect You to give me something new because You are a God who makes all things new! Because You have granted me this brand new set of 24 power-packed hours on this earth, I will use it wisely. I will use it powerfully. I will use this day audaciously. Make me a wielder of time and not just a manager of minutes. Triple my productivity, allow me to achieve more in seconds, minutes, hours, days than the average person would dare go after in a lifetime. Help me to live in the NOW. By the time night falls, I will not be exhausted, having wasted myself and my energy on fruitless pursuits. Instead, I ask to feel utterly spent, having poured out exactly what I was created to give. I will not squander this precious time that I've been granted. With Your mercy, I got this. In Your Holy Name, Amen.

Are you the master of your day or is your day happening to you and you're holding on for dear life? List the things that constantly take you off course and ask God to help you manage those interferences. Ask Him to block them for you. Make Him the master of your time, so He can make you the master of your day.

_____

_____

_____

_____

_____

_____

_____

_____

_____

_____

_____

_____

_____

_____

_____

_____

Day 23: A Prayer for Unlimited Resources

Philippians 4:19 (NIV)

And my God will meet all your needs according to the riches of his glory in Christ Jesus.

To call your goals lofty is probably the understatement of the century, but you can't help it because you're not wired to think small. The only problem is sometimes what you're going after is beyond your financial, personal or social means at that moment. So you'll need God to provide you with the tools, the money, the resources, and the connections to actually achieve what it is you're going after.

Father God, I don't know why You've given me such seemingly impossible goals, I don't know what makes me so worthy that You'd put me in charge of this grand vision. What I do know is that even though I might not see it around me, in my bank account or on my contacts just yet, everything I need is within reach. I thank You in advance for providing the resources, the finances and the people to help me make it happen. All the money I will need to see a project through from beginning to end will be in place. I thank You in advance that my well will not dry, my storehouse will be forever stocked, nothing will spoil or be eaten by pests. As endless as my ideas, so will be my resources. All the talent I need I will birth or find it in people I can count on. I thank You for putting me in the path of people I should partner with, people who can help me see Your vision through. I trust that You will pull solutions out of nowhere and that You will do it in the knick of time, on the schedule You have me on, not on the one I try so hard to manipulate. Keep me faithful to You in my time, my sacrifices and especially in my giving. I know that if I am not stingy in the things You've called me to support, You will not be stingy with me. What I love about You Father is that You live in my tomorrows as well and the tomorrows of my family. You care about my legacy and my great grandchildren that don't exist yet. Teach me to teach my children how to be good stewards so that You can trust them with the unlimited resources they will be inheriting because of my faithfulness to You. In the end, Lord God, I know full well You don't need me to give You anything, but I understand You will look at how I give as a measure of what's really in my heart. You will constantly check to see where my treasure really is and I accept that challenge. I trust that You won't leave me hanging or in the lurch, but that You'll give me the courage to step out sometimes even before You show me how the situation is going to turn out. Give me the faith to not only trust in You, but also to wait on You to deliver. For with You, all things are possible. I trust in Your Holy Name. Amen.

What do you need? Ask Him for it. Watch Him work.

_____

_____

_____

_____

_____

_____

_____

_____

_____

_____

_____

_____

_____

_____

_____

_____

_____

_____

_____

_____

_____

_____

Day 24: A Prayer to Be a Good Steward of Money

Matthew 25:23 (NIV)

"His master replied, 'Well done, good and faithful servant! You have been faithful with a few things; I will put you in charge of many things. Come and share your master's happiness!'

If you can't be trusted with money, you can't be trusted with a lot of money. It's very simple isn't it? Well, if so, why is it that when we get more, we spend more? We suddenly need things we never knew to want before we had the means. What ends up happening is that our money becomes useless and powerless except in the realm of materialism. Money is one of the great conduits of power, reach and change and we should manage it as such.

Lord, help me not to be stupid with my current money and mindless with my future wealth. Help me to see it as the currency of power, security and the catalyst for change that it is meant to be. Suppress overwhelming desires for luxury items that hold no true value. Make me a breadwinner that uses money to nourish and sustain my family for the long term. Give me long-term financial strategy that sees beyond the month's bills. Get me and keep me out of debt and in a position of inferiority because of it. Let money be attracted to me and make me wise so that I can turn a profit and reinvest. Make me an investor that sees and seeds down the road; don't let me stumble on mindless schemes for seemingly fast gains. Make me a patient amplifier of my wealth. Help me set up the future of my grandchildren by acquiring land, property, securities, and investments. Turn my new money into old money that plans to stick around for a while. Most importantly, make me a Kingdom Builder. Give me joy in adding 0's at the end of big checks. Allow my money to be the source that finances Your heavenly works on this earth. Help me build buildings and projects that change lives and turn eyes towards You. Let it be Your Name and not mine on the building. Do this not because of greed on my part, or a desire to show myself rich. But do it because in me You have planned an expensive purpose much larger than fancy houses and fast cars. Show me if I become a squanderer and teach me how to teach my children the responsibility and the maintenance of wealth. Allow me to enjoy my money by treating myself and my family with things that make them happy, but never let us forget You as the source of true joy and true prosperity. Let money be something we possess, but do not let it possess us. In Your Name, I humbly ask this most important thing. Amen.

How we handle our finances is a good reflection of how we're going to handle the authority He wants to give us. List your money issues and habits and begin the process of allowing Him to right our financial wrongs and bolster our wealth possibilities. If you're in the middle of an amazing downpour, ask Him to continue to bless You financially.

_____

_____

_____

_____

_____

_____

_____

_____

_____

_____

_____

_____

_____

_____

_____

Day 25: A Prayer for the Power to Forgive Myself

Psalm 32:5 (NIV)

Then I acknowledged my sin to you and did not cover up my iniquity. I said, "I will confess my transgressions to the LORD." And you forgave the guilt of my sin.

You're a stickler, a perfectionist, a type A personality, maybe. If you're not careful not only do you never take time to enjoy the Now and pat yourself on the back for what you have accomplished, but you often beat yourself up when you underperform and even when a situation wasn't really within your realm of control to begin with. You hold a high standard for others so when you fall short by way of unmentionable sin, you're relentless in your self-condemnation. In order to move forward and get on with repairing what needs to be repaired and to move forward in His work with a pure heart and a clear head, you have to be able to forgive yourself quickly, the same way that we are forgiven.

Father, You know the standards I hold myself to. They're higher than the ones I hold other people to and that's pretty darn high. But I've fallen short and I feel miserable, like a dirty failure. I've screwed up somehow and embarrassed myself, I feel like I've even embarrassed You. I've underperformed, under delivered and I feel like I don't deserve a second chance. But I know that You have not brought me this far to let one error or one bad judgment or my arrogant perfectionism be the death of my dreams and my destiny because that wouldn't make any supernatural sense. So please, give me the ability to see what went wrong, to understand my part in it and forgive myself for it. Help me to be as compassionate towards myself as I am with other people. I understand their hearts when they make mistakes but had the best of intentions. Help me to give myself the same benefit of the doubt I often hand out sometimes too freely to others. I'm going to mess up, it is the nature of man, help me to accept that and learn from my moments of imperfection. Don't allow guilt, harshness or unreasonable personal standards keep me from moving forward. Don't allow me to be stuck in the quagmire of failure, afraid to try again. Soothe my soul so that I comfort myself and find the strength to dust myself off, look myself in the mirror and move on. With swiftness, grant me this blessing and this ability in Jesus' name, Amen.

Write all the stuff down that you need to forgive yourself for, even the stuff for which you supposedly already forgave yourself. Determine today that this list will not be the death of you. Ask God for forgiveness and then to help you be able to let it go.

_____

_____

_____

_____

_____

_____

_____

_____

_____

_____

_____

_____

_____

_____

_____

_____

_____

Day 26: A Prayer for Supernatural Health, Physical Stamina and Will Power

Daniel 10:19 (NIV)

"Do not be afraid, you who are highly esteemed," he said. "Peace! Be strong now; be strong." When he spoke to me, I was strengthened and said, "Speak, my lord, since you have given me strength."

Isaiah 40:31 (NIV)

"But those who hope in the Lord will renew their strength. They will soar on wings like eagles, they will run and not grow weary, they will walk and not be faint."

If you think you can get to the finish line, break through the next wall and get to Level Next fatigued, out of shape and sickly you couldn't be more wrong and you will be sorely disappointed. Even if you manage to get there in bad shape, how long will you last? How long before your failing health causes you to need to take a break, to seek treatment, to take a mental retreat before breakdown ensues? Even some reasonably healthy people will wake up one day and discover they have a life-threatening illness. They will be required to stop everything and focus on survival. They will instantly have to become warriors. For the lucky rest of us, we should cherish the health we have by committing to a healthier, preventive lifestyle while we still can. If you truly are going to accomplish not just everything on your to-do list, but most importantly everything on His, you're going to need Supernatural Strength.

Father, I can feel that You have put wings on my feet. I thank You that You have given me the strength to pursue the ridiculously large dreams You've given me. I thank You that You will bless me with more than enough steam to finish the race. Give me the Godspeed to run down whomever or whatever is ahead of me, make me uncatchable to those pursuing me. Make my hands strong and give me the strength to take down giants should they dare try to stand in my way. Give me the agility to clear hurdles with finesse and efficiency. Don't let fatigue and exhaustion or depression and demoralization keep me from crossing the finish line with gas in the tank. I understand that things will be more intense the closer I get to that finish line. But I trust You will increase my energy and my physical capability as I need it. I'm blessed to have this temple. Now please give me the strength, the focus and the will power to take better care of it. I know that with what You have planned for me, there is no way I can walk into that destiny being run down, carrying too much baggage, physically and mentally. Help me desire healthier foods; give me a craving for physical activity and mental stimulation. Grant me Supernatural Endurance from the gym to the boardroom. Train me to train myself to live like a ninja, a warrior disciplined and in control of my body, my desires and my thoughts. Help me build physical and mental muscle. Since it is by Your stripes that I have been healed I don't expect to get sick much. But when I do, I expect sickness to leave as soon as it comes or at the very least, I expect to be able to carry out Your plans regardless. Give me Supernatural Energy that not only carries me but buoys those around me. Supernaturally double the effectiveness of my sleep. Make my power naps truly powerful and inexplicably restorative. Cause me to see my body as an engine that needs refueling and help me to have the will power to fuel it properly. Make me more conscious of how I treat myself and help me to take better care of this temple. Grant me rest and relaxation and recharge my battery *before* I allow myself to become depleted. Don't let me poop out! Give me more than enough fuel for the fight. Make me physically strong and formidable and help me to always use my strength for great purposes. You the Omnipotent are able to pass on Your power and I receive it in Jesus' name, Amen.

What physical and mental strongholds are holding you back? What habits are hindering your power to soar? List them and pray over them specifically. Watch God begin to give you self-control and self-discipline in spades so that you can further build your suit of armor.

_____

_____

_____

_____

_____

_____

_____

_____

_____

_____

_____

_____

_____

_____

_____

_____

Day 27: A Prayer for Wall Busting

Exodus 15:3 (NIV)

The LORD is a warrior; the LORD is his name.

Deuteronomy 3:24 (NIV)

"Sovereign LORD, you have begun to show to your servant your greatness and your strong hand. For what god is there in heaven or on earth who can do the deeds and mighty works you do?

Deuteronomy 3:22 (NIV)

Do not be afraid of them; the LORD your God himself will fight for you."

A funny thing is going to happen and it's going to irk you to no end. Right when you're on a roll, when things are going well and momentum seems to be in your corner, you'll run smack dab into a wall. For no good reason progress will stop, people and things will get in your way and it will be frustrating all the more because it won't make any logical sense. Ironically, instead of this being a bad thing, it's usually confirmation that you're well on your way to where you're supposed to be. What you're going after is so great it's actually worth it to some opposing force (in the natural or in the supernatural) to hinder you. Remember, only a worthy opponent is worthy of being opposed! In these times, you'll need to push through and pray through. In order to break through to the next level, you'll need help with wall busting from the Mighty Bulldozer Himself.

God, I'm in this situation where I know in my heart I've done what You've required of me. I've put in my work, my time, lots of energy and everything seemed to be lining up. But now, all of a sudden, I feel frozen. It feels like someone or something is blocking me without cause and that lets me know this is a job for You and from You. I'm strong but this seems to be a wall I cannot break through on my own. I am not ashamed to scream at the top of my lungs that I need You. God, thank You in advance for blowing open invisible gates that have rusted close. Break down every wall that has been built up in my pathway. My enemies are running scared and in their last ditch efforts they've constructed blockades that cannot and will not stand before You. Rejection, denial, refusal are all unwelcomed here and will not be received at this most crucial moment of my breakthrough. I know that if You be for me, not one person, thing, circumstance can dare stand against me. Help me clear hurdles that have materialized in the course of my ferocious sprinting. Give me the strength to push through relentlessly and effectively. Break down the force field of delay created by those people who are dragging their feet or fumbling things on my behalf. Speed them up, take away excuses, make it easy for them to execute Your will so that I can get on with the business of my work, my purpose and the mission You have set before me. Because You are all powerful, I know You can bust through this wall on my behalf. In Your potent name, with no doubt whatsoever I pray. Amen.

List the names of 5 walls currently in your way. Watch them crumble. Note the date.

_____

_____

_____

_____

_____

_____

_____

_____

_____

_____

_____

_____

_____

_____

_____

_____

_____

_____

_____

_____

_____

Day 28: A Prayer for the Power to Change Reality and Atmospheres

Romans 4:17 (NKJV)

As it is written, "I have made you a father of many nations" in the presence of Him whom he believed— God, who gives life to the dead and calls those things which do not exist as though they did;

1 John 5:4 (NAS)

For whatever is born of God overcomes the world. And this is the victory that has overcome the world— our faith.

Understand now that to operate in supernatural realms, you're going to need reality to change just because you demand it to. You're going to need diseases to miraculously disappear. You're going to need criminals to change their mind about attacking you right in the moment. You're going to need weather and even political events to line up with your words and plans. You're going to be surrounded by sluggish people and you're going to need them to become self-motivated worker bees. You'll not have enough money in the account and you're going to need millions to supernaturally materialize in record time. You're going to need hours to stretch and time to stand still or even speed up when you ask for it. You better believe you'll need God to help you with that.

God, You are a limitless God. So time and reality conform to You. Sometimes I am going to look out at the circumstances around me and they are not going to be conducive to what I'm trying to achieve. So I'm going to trust that I can cry out to You and You will be my "fixer", literally jumping in and changing the reality around me. Better still, Father, make me a fixer. Make me a changer of reality, mood, circumstances and atmospheres. Deadlines will need to be pushed, resources will need to be given, healing will need to be had and I'm asking that You give little old big me the power to change what's real into what must now be true. True power is walking into a room and changing the atmosphere by Your mere presence. So let the steps of my stride pack a punch. So let my words reorder set-in-stone plans, let my presence shift outcomes in Your favor and for the better. Let my smile at first flash and my handshake at first touch change minds that were already set against my plans and me. Make me literally become a game changer; industries, systems, management and governments will shift and now conform to the plans You have given me. My words and my actions will have instant, unavoidable impact. When I walk into a room moods will brighten, burdens will lighten, beliefs will be strengthened, dreams will be empowered, passions will be pursued, physical and emotional healing will happen. Let my hugs melt away shackles, freeing those who receive them from the mental prisons they've been trapped in for years. Let my prayer thoroughly, irrevocably shake loose centuries of generational bondage. In Christ's Name, I can do all these seemingly impossible things that strengthen me and all miraculous things required to carry out Your purpose. Amen.

List the hard realities that need to change in order for you to move forward from where you are? List the miracles you'd like to be a part of performing! Sit back, pray. Watch the Mountain Mover do His thing.

_____

_____

_____

_____

_____

_____

_____

_____

_____

_____

_____

_____

_____

_____

_____

_____

_____

_____

_____

Day 29: A Prayer for Undying Patience

James 1:2-8 (NKJV)

My brethren, count it all joy when you fall into various trials, knowing that the testing of your faith produces patience. But let patience have its perfect work, that you may be perfect and complete, lacking nothing.

The problem is that we want everything two yesterdays ago. That's all.

God, it seems a bit unfair that You give me a never-ending stream of goals, visions and glimpses into my destiny and then You ask me to wait for them all to come to pass. Give me the wisdom to understand that everything happens in Your perfect timing which is the best timing and that there are seasons for everything to come to pass. Give me peace when I'd rather be anxious for everything to happen right now. Instead of stewing in impatient frustration, give me the wisdom to see why the delay is occurring and help me to know how to use that seed-planting period wisely. Sometimes, I'm going to be mad at You for making me wait, determined that my timing is better than Yours. Help me to get over myself. Sometimes, I'm going to be jealous about the fact that others seem to be getting what they ask for right away or getting things I deserve. Help me to see the stupidity in comparing my story to someone else's. Often, when I feel I've been waiting too long, I'm going to start manipulating, trying to hatch plans for short cuts to get me to where I think I'm supposed to be. Help me to keep my feet still and stand still to wait for further instruction or else I might walk myself right off the path of which I'm supposed to be traveling. I'm going to need patience to deal with people as well. When we don't see eye to eye, or when they don't move as quickly as I do, or when they don't operate at the level I think is appropriate, help me to deal with those matters prudently and not harshly. Give me the power to keep my ego and my temper in check when people aren't behaving how I think they should. As well, point it out to me when I'm the real problem, when how I'm handling affairs is causing more of a problem than the issue itself. Don't allow me to be clueless and oblivious in my impatience. You have shown us patience since the beginning of time as we have continually fallen short. Yet, You love us still. Give me that capability towards my fellow humans, Your creation. Keep me grounded and give me Your unfathomable level of undying patience. In Jesus' Name, Amen.

In what areas do you need to pray seriously for patience? List them here and challenge yourself to grow a longer fuse. Look for opportunities to "practice in" patience.

_____

_____

_____

_____

_____

_____

_____

_____

_____

_____

_____

_____

_____

_____

_____

_____

_____

_____

_____

_____

Day 30: A Prayer for Humility

Proverbs 11:2 (NIV)

When pride comes, then comes disgrace, but with humility comes wisdom.

Proverbs 22:4 (NIV)

Humility is the fear of the LORD; its wages are riches and honor and life.

Once you start realizing how powerful you are, when you see how many things you seem to be manifesting just by sheer will power and the hard work of your hands, you might start to forget that you prayed for all of this to happen and that it was granted to you, not created by you. Once you're operating at the ultimate super human level, you'll have to constantly remind yourself that you didn't get their on your own. Contrary to the stories moguls like to tell, there really is no such thing as Doing It Yourself and definitely no such thing as self-made, unless you're God Himself. You'll start to read your own press and receive the recognition that's due you and instead of feeling grateful; a sense of entitlement might sneak in. This is the critical point, where things go awry for so many at the top. You'll need God's presence in order to avoid getting detrimentally too big for your britches.

Dear God, I have so much. I have achieved so many things and have seen success around every corner. I'm starting to truly feel Super Human. It's been a long time since I've missed out or messed up and it's because of this that I ask You to keep me grounded, keep me focused and aware that all of this is because of You. With every eloquent speech, remind me that You put the words in my mouth. With every skillful negotiation, remind me that You softened the hearts of the people across the table. At every step, remind me of the fact that You've always been pulling the strings, I was just obedient enough to respond to Your mighty tug. And don't let me resent that or ever want to challenge You for Your position! You've granted me unspeakable power, an abundance of talent and skill, but don't let me look at my own hands and say, "Look at what I've built!". Don't let me look in the mirror and say, "Had it not been for my attractiveness, my charm, my people skills...". Pinch me when I forget how I got to where I am right now. Pinch me hard until it bruises. Let me remind myself of Your bountiful grace, Your endless mercy and Your unreasonable favor, three things I would not have survived without. Keep me humble and willing to work alongside people who have less than me and need more than me. Keep me from an attitude that causes me to start to believe I'm the savior and remind me instead that there is only one of those and I'm not it. Remind me of the benefits of being a servant. Don't let my new found fame or fortune change my relationship with You or my family and don't let it effect the way I do business in a negative way. Don't ever let me be condescending in my charity, but remind me how, if not for a few changes in circumstances, I could easily be in a much worse position in life. Humble me low so that I might rise high. Lord God Almighty, most importantly, I ask You to strip me of everything You've ever given me if I ever start to think there's anything other than YOU serving as the wind beneath my cape. Let it be, in Your Holy incomparable name. Amen.

It's easy for our independent selves to begin to believe we've gotten where we are on our lonesome. Think back to your greatest achievements, your best moments, your most memorable awards and list how God intervened to get you there and how others played a role in your success. Then pray that God keep these remembrances top of mind as you move forward into even greater things.

_____

_____

_____

_____

_____

_____

_____

_____

_____

_____

_____

_____

_____

_____

_____

_____

_____

Day 31: A Prayer for Supernatural Protection

Psalm 91: 14-16 (NIV)

"Because he loves me," says the Lord, "I will rescue him; I will protect him, for he acknowledges my name. He will call on me, and I will answer him; I will be with him in trouble, I will deliver him and honor him. With long life I will satisfy him and show him my salvation."

You need to understand that when you start zooming along under the auspices of God Himself, during some periods it's going to feel like you have a red target squarely on your back. You're going to need it to be that even when those menacing high-beamed lasers have you locked in the crosshairs, God Himself who has personally commissioned you to do this great work of world changing will not allow the Enemy's minions to pull the trigger. In fact, the gun will be jammed and all knives pointed your way will turn dull. Since God has called you to do His work, sometimes in treacherous places and sometimes with treacherous people lurking, you will need His brand of insurance to survive the audacity of your calling. This work is not for the faint. Call on Him to cover you completely.

Dear Heavenly Father, I'm not sure I knew what I was getting into when I asked You to make me a world changer. But I asked, You listened and here I am in the middle of some serious business. Because of Your guidance, I've been effective. Because of Your power, I've been potent. Because of Your favor, I've ascended quickly. But with this elevation has come a heightened, more organized attack against me. Trouble has rushed in behind me when those powerful doors were blown open on my behalf. So I'm praying for Your Divine Coverage, the best insurance plan ever. I want the plan that makes sure I'm where I'm supposed to be at all times so that I'm under Your protection. Because of my elevation, I'm more visible now so I ask You to make me invisible to the Enemy as long as I work for You, confuse His plans against me. Help me elude the death squads that search for me when I'm working in dark regions. Jam all guns aimed at me, melt the tips of knives pointed my way, make attack dogs become my protectors, weaken the hands with plans to strangle me, make duds out of land mines, make impotent all dirty bombs. Give me a force of angels, a squadron with my name on it that goes before me and sweeps the venue, that walks beside me and guards my back. With every attempt on my life or my purpose, make me grow exponentially in power. Give me night vision and x-ray vision so that I can see danger before it sees me. Make me uncatchable, unreachable, unkillable. Make me immune to disease and if somehow I do get sick, especially when I'm traveling abroad, kill viruses quickly so I can dive back into the work at hand. Take the venom out of any snake attacks. Make all fatal poisons ineffective. Keep my family and me in an absolutely impenetrable bubble of Your making. Do not let us die in the field, but let us complete our work and when our work is done, take us up like Elijah. For You alone are able to thwart the plans of the Enemy before he makes them and because of that I call on You to keep me 77 steps ahead. Oh Righteous God who gave His only Son so that I might be protected from here into eternity, In Jesus' Name, Amen. Selah.

What are you afraid of? Tell God and watch Him eradicate both the fear and the threat.

_____

_____

_____

_____

_____

_____

_____

_____

_____

_____

_____

_____

_____

_____

_____

_____

_____

_____

_____

Forever: Psalm 91

Whoever dwells in the shelter of the Most High
will rest in the shadow of the Almighty.
2 I will say of the Lord, "He is my refuge and my fortress,
my God, in whom I trust."

3 Surely he will save you
from the fowler's snare
and from the deadly pestilence.
4 He will cover you with his feathers,
and under his wings you will find refuge;
his faithfulness will be your shield and rampart.
5 You will not fear the terror of night,
nor the arrow that flies by day,
6 nor the pestilence that stalks in the darkness,
nor the plague that destroys at midday.
7 A thousand may fall at your side,
ten thousand at your right hand,
but it will not come near you.
8 You will only observe with your eyes
and see the punishment of the wicked.

9 If you say, "The Lord is my refuge,"
and you make the Most High your dwelling,
10 no harm will overtake you,
no disaster will come near your tent.
11 For he will command his angels concerning you
to guard you in all your ways;
12 they will lift you up in their hands,
so that you will not strike your foot against a stone.
13 You will tread on the lion and the cobra;
you will trample the great lion and the serpent.

14 "Because he loves me," says the Lord, "I will rescue him;
I will protect him, for he acknowledges my name.
15 He will call on me, and I will answer him;
I will be with him in trouble,
I will deliver him and honor him.
16 With long life I will satisfy him
and show him my salvation."

About the Author:

Jade Simmons

Rockstar Concert Pianist & Emergence Expert

How do you get to be named Classical Music's *"No.1 Maverick"*? By repeatedly defying expectations, delivering riveting performances and combining passion and innovation at every turn. Called a "musical force of nature", Jade Simmons is easily one of the most exciting and versatile artists on the scene today. For her work on and away from the stage, *Essence* magazine featured Jade alongside First Lady Michelle Obama and Olympic gold medalist Gabby Douglas as a part of their *Style & Substance* List which highlights women who have expanded the definition of beauty and achievement. Additionally, she has been recognized two years in a row by Symphony Magazine, listed as one of *Ebony* magazine's *Top 30 Leaders under 30* (2008) and named Houston's *Best Arts Ambassador* by the Houston Press. She made waves as one of the rare classical artists invited to perform at the taste making South by Southwest Festival where her show was ultimately branded one of the *"Best of SXSW 2014"*. For the highly anticipated *What Happened, Miss Simone?*, a documentary on the legendary Nina Simone, Jade performs selections by Chopin, Debussy and Bach for the footage highlighting Simone's early Classical beginnings. The film premiered January 2015 at the Sundance Film Festival. As founder of the *School of Emergence,* Jade coaches and trains creative women with entrepreneurial ambition to turn their creativity into clear income and their passion into profitable enterprise.

A native of Charleston, South Carolina, Jade's childhood in the low country included arts, sports, academics and church-related activities. She's the daughter of civil rights activist Jerome Smalls and Loretta Smalls, the praying mother whose career has been in higher education administration. Loretta also served as keyboardist and one of the ministers of music at Abundant Life Church where Jade and eventually her little sister Isis were avid members of the church's youth group. An unusually gifted talent in her hometown, Jade went on to pursue her undergraduate work in piano performance at Northwestern University. While there, she would become Miss Chicago, Miss Illinois and ultimately first runner-up at the 2000 Miss America Pageant with a platform of Youth Suicide Prevention. This would take her at the age of 21 to testify in front of Congress on behalf of Mental Health Funding and later be a part of the rollout of Surgeon General Satcher's *National Strategy to Prevent Suicide*. In 2003, Ms. Simmons received her Master's degree in Piano Performance under acclaimed pianist Jon Kimura Parker at Rice University in Houston, TX. While in Houston with her high school sweetheart turned husband, Jahrell, she took a job as a church pianist and youth pastor for a small Baptist church and had no idea how this ministerial role would come back to meet her later in her career.

As an uncommon artist, Jade's committed to expanding the boundaries of Classical music and its presentation. Today, she offers an incredibly diverse mix of repertoire from the Classics to the cutting edge and audiences have come to expect creative projects backed by riveting performances. Ms. Simmons has toured the US extensively in recital and with orchestra highlighted by performances at venues as wide-ranging as Ravinia, the

Chicago Sinfonietta in Symphony Hall, New York's Town Hall, the Detroit Institute of Arts, The White House and she received the Sphinx Organization's Medal of Excellence in a concert held at the US Supreme Court hosted by Justice Sonia Sotomayor. Jade's multiple talents make her a true Renaissance woman of the millennium taking her in the direction of *#1 Amazon Best-Selling Author* for her new book *Audacious Prayers for World Changers*, arts presenter, coach/consultant, professional speaker, webcast host for the Van Cliburn International Piano competition and she writes about the arts for the *Huffington Post*. An advocate for emerging artists, she teaches a graduate level course on Artist Career Development in the University of Houston's Program in Arts Leadership. Today, she also embraces the role of serving on the leadership team of the women's ministry at Christian Tabernacle Church in Houston where she spearheads the new *Divinely Aligned* Women's Seminar and is the author of the soon to be released *Power. Passion. Purpose!* Bible study. For more inspiration, information and entertainment, visit the all new JadeSimmons.com.

If you loved *Audacious Prayers*, sign up at www.jadesimmons.com for a FREE MP3 of selected prayers read aloud by Jade. Download the full audio version today on Amazon and take these powerful prayers with you everywhere you go!

Follow @JadeSimmons for endless audacity

Watch EmergenceTV on
www.Facebook.com/JadeSimmons

Praise for Audacious Prayers

"In Audacious Prayers, Jade has given us words to meditate and pray daily for the next thirty-one days. It's a way to forever change our lives by connecting the dreamer and visionary within us to the God who first gives, and then fulfills our dreams and visions."

Senior Pastor Dr. R. Heard
Christian Tabernacle (Houston, Texas)
ctab.org
@praywithpastor

"It's amazing to meet a woman of faith who truly has it all. Jade is not only an accomplished visionary leader, she is a spiritual dynamo! Her God-given ability to guide women as they navigate the journey of the unknown with audacious faith is second to none. Prayer is certainly powerful. In *Audacious Prayers*, Jade teaches us to take prayer to an entirely new level. She reminds us that all things truly are possible. We serve an audacious God who has called us to live an audacious life! Don't just read this book - be it."

Marshawn Evans Daniels, The Godfidence Coach
Reinvention Strategist™
Godfidence® Institute & Business School
Believe Bigger. Live Bigger™
Peak Performance & Faith Mastery
marshawnevans.com
@marshawnevans

"*Audacious Prayers for World Changers: Live and Pray Out Loud* is a timeless and priceless contribution for all generations, denominations, and people of faith who dare to believe, pray, and DO the word of God. As a publisher, a lot of books about faith cross my desk. But this is the rare one that could literally serve as a manual on how to live an audacious lifestyle."

Dr. Fred Jones Speaks
Amazon Best Selling Author
Speaker | Professor | Attorney
drfredjones.com
@fredjonesspeaks

"*Audacious Prayers for World Changers* is more than a book of prayers, it's the very language of God written in a way that helps business owners communicate with the Father more effectively for those things that concern them and their enterprises. I love the strategic alignment of the prayers to cover all the areas that business owners need encouragement in. This book brings so much hope and liberty for the 21st Century CEO, the people that are called to change the world through business enterprise!"

LaShawne Holland, America's Wealth Activator & Queen of Green
Facebook: LaShawne Holland – Financial Coach
www.lashawneholland.com
@LashawneHolland

"Jade Simmons captures the exact heart and voice of every visionary leader and entrepreneur who dares to believe God for the impossible in her new book *Audacious Prayers for World Changers*. It is the missing link for anyone seeking to live and lead beyond their own strengths and are trusting God to move in a big way. The first time I began to read through each prayer, tears literally fell from my eyes because it was the first time I'd ever seen the desires and silent prayers of my heart so eloquently expressed in writing. I finally felt like I had a go-to resource for inspiration and clarity that was a direct reflection of the audacious faith that resides inside me."

Melissa J. Nixon
Executive Leadership Coach, Speaker, & Courageous Life Mentor
courageouslifeacademy.com
@melissajnixon

Read more at www.jadesimmons.com